Three
Golden Pearls
on a String

Three Golden Pearls on a String

The Esoteric Teachings of Karate-Do and the Mystical Journey of a Warrior Priest

by

Thomas M. White

North Atlantic Books
Berkeley, California

Three Golden Pearls on an String:
The Esoteric Teachings of Karate-Do
and the Mystical Journey of a Warrior Priest

Published by North Atlantic Books
            2800 Woolsey Street
            Berkeley, California 94705

Brush paintings and calligraphy by Thomas M. White
Cover and book design by Paula Morrison
Typeset in Palladium by Classic Typography

Printed in the United States of America

Three Golden Pearls on an String: The Esoteric Teachings of
Karate-Do and the Mystical Journey of a Warrior Priest is spon-
sored by the Society for the Study of Native Arts and Sciences, a
nonprofit educational corporation whose goals are to develop an
educational and crosscultural perspective linking various scien-
tific, social, and artistic fields; to nurture a holistic view of arts,
sciences, humanities, and healing; and to publish and distribute
literature on the relationship of mind, body, and nature.

DEDICATION

Three Golden Pearls on a String is dedicated to Master Eizo
Shimabuku, who first exposed me to traditional Karate-do;
to Shihan Tsutomu Ohshima who impressed upon me the
spiritual value of Karate-do and its practical application in contemporary society; to Albert G. Vandenberg who reminds me
still of my own vanity and the journey that lies ahead; to those
seniors and juniors who maintain their confidence in, and carry
the torch of goodwill and right-human relationships; and to
the martial artists of all forms and systems who would dare
move beyond the rigid structures that separate our brotherhood
into a common field of service to one humanity.

Thomas M. White
February 1986
Berkeley, California

The warrior is also a priest . . .

PREFACE

After nearly 23 years of karate practice, I still have questions and concerns about its function in contemporary society. While it is easy to relate to the mental and physical disciplines ascribed to karate training, exactly what is the true Tao of karate when referred to as Karate-do? If it is true, as generally believed, that karate was an art developed and taught at the Shaolin Monastery in northern China by one Bodhidharma, a Buddhist monk, then karate as we practice it today would appear to be void of one of the most sacred and essential aspects of its composite body of knowledge—Its esoteric teachings.

I have had the great fortune to study under exemplary teachers who, as good teachers, have precipitated a life-long quest far transcending our momentary existence as physical beings on this earth plane: Eizo Shimabuku, Tsutomu Ohshima and Guru Dorjie, my Yoga Master. They have each added to my still evolving understanding of the true nature of Being, and my concept of karate-do as a valid method of spiritual and psychic development; thus, leading me to explore the art beyond its more apparent mechanical applications and truly adopt it as a path of spiritual unfoldment.

Those more essential and transcending elements of karate, which color my philosophical approach to the art, are the basis for this work; *Three Golden Pearls on a String* . . .

Thomas M. White

FOREWORD

Budo is the way to cut oneself from one's first step to the point one can reach. To cut oneself means to face our own mind directly, honestly, strictly; to polish the mind by cutting away cowardliness, selfishness, ugliness, and weakness.

To have the mind's eye, we must have a strong mind. At the same time, it is absolutely necessary to be very humble.

Mr. Thomas White is not only a gifted person with a strong mind and body but he also has this very important humbleness. I believe that his own expressions become seeds for the younger seekers' minds that are following him. I also believe that real harmony of mankind will be brought only by the leaders' strongwill seeking the way with humbleness.

Tsutomu Ohshima

INTRODUCTION
TO THE SECOND EDITION

Thanks to Richard Grossinger and North Atlantic Books, I have the opportunity to amend some aspects of the first text, and add additional information which I hope will provide the reader more insight in to the esoteric gleanings of martial arts training. These writing are intended to remind each, practitioner, regardless of rank or system that physical activity is a result and not a cause. Intent and perception summarize both our individual and collective actions.

Three Golden Pearls on a String is an attempt to simplify the concepts of Karate-do—to move the art out of its narrow definitions, which are often synonymous with systems, better technique, and tradition, into the whole of life. The emphasis of this book is on relations. It is about our relationships with ourselves, with other human beings and with the environment. It has been written in acknowledgement to and in appreciation of those who train, who teach, and who continue to grow in the knowledge that we are each polishing our preexisting mirrors in order to reflect more clearly the vision of our Souls.

The effort made has been to reflect the sort of innocent purity that is embodied in basics . . . a single kick or punch delivered with total concentration and commitment. This kind of attack, though it may not be effective in the beginning stages of one's practice, is honest. It represents simplicity and efficiency.

As karma could only dictate, I recently met an individual who was reestablishing her own "center" by writing kanji. I suggested that she read my manuscript and express the feelings she got in single characters. In reflecting on her work, she indicated that she needed more practice ... my sentiments exactly: Though I have been practicing over 26 years, I still need more practice. I recognize this need as a professional who works with people, it shows up in my personal relationships, and I see it again when I think of the difficulties we face as a world community. By mutual consent, and in the spirit of practice, I am introducing in the kanji of Yukari Wada.

Thomas M. White

Three
Golden Pearls
on a String

Through the subtleness of weaving, the many threads of a precious garment seem as one fabric.

Such is the nature of the TAO.

THE INSTRUCTIONS

The essence of karate-do, along with its many forms representing its cohesive body of knowledge, has been passed down through the ages from master to disciple. Though the footprints of those ancient masters who developed and passed on the many secrets of the art have been erased from the sands of time, the seeds they planted have taken root and become strong trees with many branches.

> A single thread strings together the
> three golden pearls of wisdom; each pearl
> a step on the path leading from man to
> master; each joined to the other by the
> all encompassing force of life. They
> manifest one as the student, one as the
> instructor, and one as the instructions.

"The one Universal Light, which to Man is Darkness, is ever existent."

—The Chaldean Book of Numbers

The TAO is not an option; we have
only the choice of method. The method
that one applies dictates the circum-
stances one will encounter upon the path.
To master the art of karate requires
much training. Yet, the mastery of karate
is not in and of itself the way. Karate is
but a tool that the masters have found
valuable in cultivating the spirit of the
worthy mechanic. The realization of one's
true nature is to make manifest the art of
life. This art is what allows one the most
and best creative application of all tools.

Upon entering the temple gate, I bowed with anticipation before soliciting the instructions of the master. "I would like to join your class," I stated, after being introduced by one of the senior black belts. "For what reason do you come?" the master asked. "I have come to learn the art of self-defense," I replied—as if in the question, the answer was also contained. "And which self do you wish to defend?" He responded as if still the question had not been answered.

Okinawa, July 1963

It was six months before we spoke again . . . though I saw him daily, thereafter. Each day of painful zazen on the concrete courtyard beyond the heavy iron gate which served as the Okinawan Headquarters of the All Japan Karate-do League, prompted the question: **Which self is worthy of defending?**

The seeker on the path, for self's sake,
must first understand the non-self; what
is real and what is illusion; what is eternal and what will pass with time.

In youth, one frolics for the joy of
frolic; as an adult, one aspires to ensure
a secure future; in old age, one yields to
the inevitability of death. Not knowing,
some still ask: "Who am I, and what
worth is Life?" A fish taken from the
stream soon dies. The stream, however,
continues on to the river, and the river
to the sea.

5

Change can not be avoided; it is a natural process—birth and death are part of that process, but are distinct from living and dying.

Humanity, as an organic phenomena, is both living and dying simultaneously. But unlike birth and death, living and dying imply a certain awareness of "being."

Karate is not separate from work, family or society. What is its merit without meditation? In the scheme of evolution, which is the greater task—to control the body, or to control the mind? There is, after all, a distinction between the chariot and the charioteer.

Between birth and death there is living and dying. Birth is a mechanical process; living is the creative activity of the soul. Dying is the yielding of the spirit to the greater will of nature; death is withdrawal into the sacred womb—the reconciliation of human choice and cosmic function.

It was early evening when I passed through the squeaky iron gates leading into the dojo, passing beneath the hand-carved sign which proposed the mystical Greek axiom: "Man, Know Thy Self!"

Vanity is the strangest of teachers. Of itself, it is not rational. It cannot accept the differences between what it is and what it is not; it continually wages a war between what is and what it wishes to be, and it pretends to be what it can't become—the truth.

"Those who have attained perfect renunciation are free from any sense of duality; they are unaffected by likes and dislikes, Arjuna, and are free from the bondage of self-will. The immature think that knowledge and action are different, but the wise see them as the same. The person who is established on one path will attain the rewards of both. The goal of knowledge and the goal of service are the same; those who fail to see this are blind."

—*The Bhagavad Gita*

> It is an unwritten code: One must struggle that defeat never comes from within—for, it is not the fault of the arrow if the aim of the archer is untrue.

"If its application is for a good purpose, then the art is of great value; but if it is misused, then there is no more evil or harmful art than karate."

—*Karate-Do Kyohan*

Aspire to understand aggression. It is a natural enemy to the harmonious course of the spirit; it creates anxiety, and distorts clear vision and unbiased perception. The wind is not aggressive, nor is the sea. As a windstorm, or as a tidal wave, neither is aggressive. Even the tiger responds only in accordance with its nature.

It is a misleading philosophy to consider karate-do a way of aggression. No, it is not the art that is aggressive; it is the temperament of the artist that often leads to misunderstanding.

Defense is the main goal of the martial arts, and the understanding of the essential self.

It was a very clear evening as we practiced the form Chinto in the open courtyard beneath a full moon, when the Master approached me for the first time during training. He watched for what seemed an unending moment, then assumed the cat-stance characteristic of the opening move of the kata and said, "I will teach you."

Of all things to remember in the dynamics of practice, one should remember that posture is also an attitude. No matter how well one performs, without the right attitude one cannot grasp the significance of Karate-do—one polishes the shell only, without the knowledge of the pearl within.

"The grass may wither, but the roots die not
And when spring comes it renews its full life;
Only grief, so long as its roots remain,
Even without spring, is of itself reborn.
                    —Ch'en Shan-Min, Sung Dynasty

Pain is the first lesson of a warrior—
the pain of diligent training and self-less
reflection on the essential dharma of the
Tao. The second lesson is aloneness,
wherein the true identity is unveiled and
the path becomes a true friend and a
heavy burden; in aloneness, the discom-
forts of a world humanity stand revealed.
The third lesson is compassion from
which the warrior recognizes that he is
also a priest, and that brotherhood is not
a condition which we must ponder—
rather, a reality we must accept. All
things are eternally one.

The Moon Cannot Be Stolen

Ryokan, a Zen master, lived the simplest kind of life in a little hut at the foot of a mountain. One evening a thief visited the hut only to discover there was nothing in it to steal.

Ryokan returned and caught him. "You may have come a long way to visit me," he told the prowler, "and you should not return empty-handed. Please take my clothes as a gift."

The thief was bewildered. He took the clothes and slunk away.

Ryokan sat naked, watching the moon. "Poor fellow," he mused, "I wish I could give him this beautiful moon."

—*Zen Flesh, Zen Bones*

Tradition is not always sacred. It is
sometimes flawed by social and cultural
complexities quite inappropriate for the
journey to be taken.

Tradition is of value only to the extent
that it embodies those essential elements
that address and appreciate the universal-
ity of the Tao. Tradition for the sake of
tradition is a hindrance to wisdom. Tradition is a strong tree with deep roots,
and one must understand its nature to
appreciate its fruit.

The cherry blossom has for years been
a symbol of beauty and purity. Still, the
acorn thrives—and the oak tree.

This is also true of man. It is the evolution of his spirit that is of essential importance, and not tradition—except that
tradition is functional, to the "warrior"
it is not expedient.

In training, nothing is ever repeated. Each lesson is different from all other lessons, each moment is fleeting. The same technique performed 1,000 times is different each time . . . all similarity is but memory.

Constant training creates a particular rhythmic momentum which embodies an idea of perfection.

Strenuous training when correctly applied is good for the body and the spirit. But "right" training is vital to the development of a functional warrior. To overlook the basic precepts of karate-do is to deny earth while seeking heaven.

And what right does one have to look forward to achieving in another world that which one will not strive to attain in this?

Basics are the keys to understanding the simplest elements of our own complex natures. Existence, however, is not complicated; it is only confused. In karate-do every form, no matter how advanced, is still but a series of basic movements. In life, every crisis—no matter how drastic—has a simple solution.

Strenuous training should be designed to forge physical and mental vehicles sufficiently developed to support the intensity of the spirit's will, to endure in its radiant innocence, and to know love as an end to all sorrow.

One million arrows launched from the
Many bows of an army of men
So many souls lost in battle
Weeping widows wail
Strong men cry
Children sing songs of patriotism
They do not understand yet . . .
That the blood shed is real

We must come to realize our oneness
with nature, and our common enemy—
fear.

The path is one of change, and our ability to adapt to the conditions that change
brings about.

THE INSTRUCTOR

Sooner or later the true seeker
will graduate from the Cosmos
of minor mysteries—*questions of
personal enlightenment, etc.*—
into the Cosmos of greater
mysteries which in some ways
resembles a vast hierarchy of Beings.
—Guru Dorjie

I arrived early for Saturday morning training. It was August. The smooth cement of the outdoor gymnasium would be scorching by 10:00; changing clothes on the narrow porch leading to the main living quarters of the Master's dwelling would be the only respite from the heat.

Approaching the fading gray gate, half open to the winding roadway, I heard a strange, unfamiliar monotone coming from behind the closed teak and rice paper doors that screened the porch from the traditional part of the household: "Aum Mani Padme Hum" . . . accented by intermittent grinding sounds . . . prayer beads.

> The "Way" is forever inward. It is not separate from religion; it is religion in its most high form. To separate the "Way" from religion is to separate thought from reality.
>
> Through our thinking we become.
> Through our actions we express that which we are becoming.
>
> Pride and vanity are attachments to the outer embellishments of the path. They are useless garments which must be burned away by the inner fires of realization.

I entered the iron gates everyday for 12 months until the time of departing, which was but another beginning. I said thank you, he said, "Go in peace." The group sang together for the last time the karate song: "There is no first attack in karate, karate is a way of humility and service and love and good-will . . ."

"What self do you defend?"

—Shimabuku, Eizo, Ju-Dan

Teaching is not the Tao, the Tao can
only be known by learning. Teachers
are but one pearl on a sacred string. Not
for themselves, but of themselves must
they give.

The warrior-priest is an unpretentious
model, a signpost upon which the words
of the heart have been written.

"These rules are written only for those to whom I give my peace; those who can read what I have written with inner as well as the outer sense."

—H.P. Blavatsky, *Light On The Path*

Wisdom is not a commodity; it cannot be bargained for in the marketplace. It cannot be sold, and should never be an item of contract. Wisdom is attained only by individual effort, and comes in its own time and fashion. Even knowledge must be given with caution—after much consideration has been tended to its application and its effects upon both its recipient and the social order.

It should not be the purpose of the instructor to create an exclusive society, but to help individuals realize their greater function within the society in which they exist.

The real virtue of training is found on uncommon ground, in those moments of darkness when victory is attained, though defeat seemed inevitable.

Karate is not something that one does, it is something that one becomes. And though the external mask of training might be readily seen in the lighted arena, the essence of Karate-do is ever the veiled presence of being.

True warriors dare to live as they believe; to be true to their most noble dreams; to understand and control the raging tides of their emotions; to perceive their indivisibility with nature, and follow the course dictated by their spirits.

". . . Baso asked: 'What do you seek?' 'Enlightenment,' replied Daiju. 'You have your own treasure house. Why do you seek outside?' Baso asked . . ."
Open Your Own Treasure House, *Zen Flesh, Zen Bones*

The true teacher first becomes a warrior. The true warrior acquires the nature of a priest. It is in the mind that the body is trained, and in devotion that the mind is trained.

It is ultimately wasteful to have a good slave and a poor slavemaster.

In the early days of karate training on the Ryuku Islands, post 1945, there were no distinct ryus (schools). It was not uncommon for a student to seek instructions from several masters during the course of training. Though the art was practiced in relative obscurity, teachers understood their limitations based upon their specialized training and encouraged students to expand their knowledge by formal introductions to other noted instructors in the close-knit brotherhood. The art, not the ego, was at stake!

Each teacher is provided two types
of students: Those who understand and
follow the way; and those who follow
the way but do not understand it. Those
who understand and follow the way
must be given the freedom of creative
expression—they are new vines on an old
tree, and will bear their fruit in a season
yet to come.

Those who follow the way, but do not
understand, must be given stern direction—they are old vines which cling to
maintain the quality of the fruit until
the new season is realized.

A good teacher must know how and
when to prune each vine, understanding the seasons of growth and the seasons of harvest.

According to numerical equations developed by certain mystical sects, Karate means to awaken or to become enlightened and has a numerical value of twenty. As such, karate-do could be translated as the path, or the way of enlightenment.

The dojo is also a place of worship. Therein is maintained the spirit of the teachings, and an atmosphere is preserved wherein the student might be vulnerable without the fear of vulnerability.

Karate politics are daring adventures into the dark ages and cannot escape the pit-falls of any other political system which seeks to control the minds and hearts of its servants.

Those who would declare themselves masters should seek guidance, thereafter, in the hearts of those who would become students.

The essence of teaching is one's continued training. Karate-do is not a philosophy, it is a practice. It is not rank and grading, it is living and sharing. It is not a way of war, but ultimately a way of peace and reconciliation.

The instructor must realize the many
approaches to the foot of the mountain,
and the many paths to the top.

It is not responsible to take an army
into war and know nothing of the ene-
mies which one will engage, or the ter-
rain upon which the battle will be fought.

It was a difficult task . . . seeking guidance upon the path! For
one having fought in the sociopolitical and religious wars on the
streets of the inner cities of America, detachment and private
training sessions were realistic options. There was one other
option though: Shotokan Karate of America. It was not, however, the sharpness of the sword that attracted me . . . no, it
was the character of the swordsman. I could call him "Master."

At the heart of each "way" there exists
a shrine constructed by those who have
journeyed before.

Take no path for granted—respect each
for the wisdom it contains.

Often in the temple, least auspicious,
the greatest knowledge is revealed.

Be, then, cautious upon the path and
reflect upon this ancient riddle: One can
attain knowledge and still be far from
the truth.

There is an inner and outer form. Each must be studied and made a part of the total learning experience. It is the task of the instructor to assist the student in gaining a more clear perspective of the selfless self and its unlimited potential.

THE STUDENT

The end of training is the top of a mountain which one can never reach without finding still another mountain to be climbed.

Though the seeds of knowledge may be planted, they will not yield an abundant crop without nourishment. Even after the hull erupts and the young plant forces its way through the soil, there is still the need to tend it faithfully while its roots grow strong and the first signs of fruit are realized. Even then, there will be the need to constantly manicure the branches and till the soil.

There is no easy way to perfection in Karate-do. Even at the peak of mastery, there is the need for constant refining of perception.

"You must train every day," the Master reminded. . . . "the body and the mind must be of one accord."

Choose with great care the one you would aspire to learn from, and then commit yourself to learning. There should be no breaks between one practice and another, only the application of concept in differing arenas. This is the key to realizing the value of "bushido" in contemporary society, and understanding strategy.

Imagination is a critical faculty; it must be developed to the finest degree. Through imagination, one becomes expressive and acquires intuition.

"All things are in the mind!"

—Guru Dorjie, A.G.V.

A good weapon is only the timely extension of one's ma-ai. It simply fills a vacuum in time and space. It does not have to be destructive, but it must be relative. Great strength must be tempered by a greater compassion. Only then can we realize the tranquility of the still moon on a dark night.

In 1969 I was ordained, linking mentally my physical and emotional experiences sufficiently to realize there was no self to defend. There was no need for internal argument; nature is impersonal. The sun shines upon the face of humanity without bias.

When one is under sound attack one
must die, and yet live, from moment to
moment. It is in momentary living that
one is free from distraction, and finds
victory through a silence which contains
the only possible solution—right action.

Zazen is not just a way to open and
close a training session. It is the Alpha
and Omega of the art, and of the human
drama . . .

It takes practice to still the mind. And,
what is meditation except mediation between the self and the selfless self!

極致

The student must be patient! It takes
only one arrow to pierce the heart of
the target, yet it takes countless hours
of training to learn to draw the bow
correctly.

I worked with many young people on the streets of the city
and in camps high in the mountains. Youth understand the
intensity of the moment, but cannot conceive tomorrow. Tomorrow is a worthy opponent that may never come . . . still
the warrior prepares.

Sacrifice is not a part of the "Way," it is the "Way." Training is not a part of Karate-do, it is Karate-do. Training is not to defeat the enemy, but to establish an identity with a self which transcends the mechanical nature of material contemplations.

. . . sacrifice is not vain self-torture to reach some ideal state of being; it is but a choice of action consistent with one's priorities.

Timing and rhythm are related. In training, one must learn to change one's rhythm while maintaining a sense of timing—otherwise, one's movements will be empty and one's defense weak.

If one has based a lifetime of training upon defense, one has already imagined his defeat. If one's life is rooted in action, defense becomes a natural variable in the scheme of things.

Too often in kata, we imagine a motionless mark. Though the practitioner moves, the targets remain as wooden dummies waiting to be attacked. Kata is good for the development of rhythm. To develop timing takes a moving target and the ability to adjust and readjust one's own dynamics, based on the variations in the movement.

It is obvious, then, at some level of training one's kata changes based upon the perception of one's opponents. It's daring, yes; but it is not unrealistic to assume.

This is, of course, a different philosophy from the traditional maintenance of an art form. But, isn't it within scope of the art? Translation of Kata is a relatively recent phenomena. In kata, each of the "inventors" expressed their particular understanding and approach to offense and defense as applied to real or imaginary combat situations. If this is so, have there been any changes in our approach to combat in the last two centuries? Of course there have . . .

Fate is still the dominant factor in life. In training one learns to accommodate destiny, and with purpose meet fate as an ally that offers greater knowledge. One's destiny is not in the hands of the instructor. One must, with diligence, practice the "Tao" for one's own benefit and that of the greater society. But one must pay proper respect to the teacher as part of the learning experience, and sharing in the work at hand. It is never enough that the teacher is prepared to teach; it is also essential that the student is prepared to learn.

I thought myself to mimic the master's expressions and thereby study the nature of his internal dialogue. It was one way to cultivate my imagination. It was not enough, however, to take upon myself his character. The essence of the path was to refine my own.

In training, basics should be practiced
in two distinct ways: One for precise
technical understanding, the other with
an abandoned spirit. Only then can we
join the two extremes of theory and
application.

All mechanical apparatuses have their
limitations—these must be understood.
But they also have their range of active
expression—this must be imagined. Else-
wise, we impose severe limitations where
we could experience unlimited freedom!

The magic of training is in the exploration of its creative potential

Kata is a lesson in strategy. There are three ways to practice kata: Slow for technique and transition; medium for visualization and rhythm; fast for focus and penetration.

In all cases, however, there must be a conscious effort to relate to the dual nature of the given form. Each has a peculiar rhythm, strategy, and technique based upon the actions of an imagined opponent and one's response in attack, counter attack, or defense. The key to kata is the correct understanding of transitory postures and attitudes. One must be able to relate to the strength of the opponent, perceive his height and weight, and sense his strengths and weaknesses.

As one progresses in kata, one's opponents become more technically sophisticated, and one gradually adjusts to meet this greater challenge.

". . . And Victory am I; and Earnestness; and Determination; and the Truth . . ."
—*The Bhagavad Gita* on Universal Perfection

It is sometimes wise to retreat. Yet in
times of retreat, let not the reason be due
to the flight of the arrow—let it rather
be the nature of the archer.

Winning is a rather redundant explanation for having achieved a specific task; often without consideration for the value of the actions taken.

A teacher of mysticism once told me: "One must act for the sake of the action alone. The reward for the act is contained, already, in the power of its expression."

In reaching out for an opponent, one
encounters the void. To pass through this
void and successfully engage the opponent requires a great degree of abandoned control and confidence. It is the
space between the tip of sword when
drawn, and the target when struck.

In zazen, imagine a triangle. One point at the ajna, the brow
chakra; the second point the svadishthana, the chakra situated
at the base of the genital organ; the third point the target. A
fourth plane is imagined from the Anahata Chakra in the region
of the heart or cardiac plexus; centering point one and point
two, leading directly to point three. The object: To deliberately
move from the base to the point of triangle with increased
momentum and velocity.

. . . an offensive attitude!

One must see life through the eyes of a
warrior to understand the resolve of the
tornado and the peaceful calm which
follows.

One must respond, not react, to crisis . . .

If one reacts to a strong opponent, it is much too late. Timely
response requires the cultivation of a degree of sensitivity, allowing one to perceive the ensuring storm even before the first
rains have fallen.

One must either push or pull one's opponent, entering into his ma-ai or allowing him to enter into one's own.

In pushing, it is important to reflect upon one's approach, forcing an opening in the opponent's defensive attitude.

In pulling, one must mirror the opponent's attack, allowing him to extend himself without the possibility of safe retraction.

In either case, the hara must be alive and there must not be physical nor mental stagnation.

When thinking of approaching or being approached, it might be of help to imagine a rectangle—the four outer points being the extreme points of the hips, and parallel points of each shoulder. A parallel line, drawn from the top of the head to the base of the spine, provides a center line. The center line is critical in formulating strategy.

. . . an approach to defensive strategy.

The elbows and shoulder should work
together, much like the knees and ankles.
There is a trilogy in either: The hips,
elbows, and fists; and the hips, knees,
and feet.

In 1972, or thereabout, I had an opportunity to participate
in an exchange practice at Cal-Tech in Los Angeles. On the
seventh day of a fast, I still had the fortune to take first place
in the kumite competition. A week later, Ohshima Sensei pre-
sented me with a treasured piece of calligraphy which he had
prepared. He intimated: "I am sorry we had no trophies, but
I would like to give you this." For several years I studied the
character of the kanji—Keigo: "Respect and honor." I adopted
the character as my personal logo and have tried to devise my
training methods to reflect its significance.

It is often easy to get lost in the theory of straight lines versus circles. The logic of either seems simple: Straight lines must ultimately curve. Curves ultimately become straight lines at the point of impact. Those who expound the straight line without the ability to "return" are as vulnerable as those who expound the curve without the sense of penetration. Which is best is determined by the nature of the evolving circumstance. In close encounters, there is often the need for small circular motions; using the hips and shoulder as pivot points, keeping the knees and ankles relaxed—the weapons short and ripping, rather than straight.

Such attacks and/or counter attacks provide the least restricted approaches to vital target areas, maximum leverage, and the greatest range of motion.

To close the distance between oneself and one's opponent (entering and exiting the void), the straight line often proves the most effective strategy. Either theory, however, depends upon momentary relationships which evolve during the course of an encounter. A brief dialogue in perceptual awareness can summarize this concept: When traveling, determine the route which allows for the safest journey, and don't take unnecessary risks.

. . . expect the unexpected!

After practicing kata for 23 years, there is only one thing that I am sure of: Most practitioners vaguely practice and understand only one-half of any given form.

Kata has a wide range of applications.
It would be a mistake to confine them all
to the smooth, constant atmosphere of the
training hall. Why not suppose that some
were for fighting at night, others for
close quarters, some for sandy beaches,
and others for unrestricted spaces. It's
worth thinking about. Another thought:
Kata contains the strategy of various
systems of thought and are designed to
help the student relate to a variety of offensive strategies and defensive attitudes.

While we mostly practice the offensive
strategies, more or less, we seldom relate
to the defensive attitudes of the many
imaginary opponents we slay during kata
practice.

We must at some point change our emphasis and examine the other half of
the kata.

Kata was developed so an individual could practice alone. They are, however, most effective when two or more persons practice as a team . . . some attacking, some defending.

One should not forget to practice deep
slow breathing, gaining therefrom a
deeper sense of body-mind integration
and sensual perception.

Shadows upon a quiet lake are but
reflections, even though the war on the
distant shore rages in its intense brutal-
ity. One is the nature of the mind; one is
the temperament of the spirit.

I can remember the master saying, "It is like walking; it's just like you walk." Transitions from one stance to another should be natural . . .

There are many schools of thought about stances. They are all basic. What is important is that there are not great distinctions in the transitions from one stance to another. The feet should be the approximate distance in the front-stance that they are in the horse-stance or back-stance, and the body stable. The cat-stance is a notable exception, yet evolves around the same center as do other postures. And I might add, it is based on the same principles of movement fluidity. Stances accommodate a variety of weapons systems. The low front stance, for example, was initially developed as a defensive posture. The higher, more natual front stance was more appropriate for offensive startegies.

In the practice of kicking, it is of prime importance that the hips rotate freely and the back remain as vertical as possible. The hara acts as a gyroscope.

In front-kicks, the power must not be compromised by "throwing" the foot. There should be a smooth, flowing motion without the feeling of separation between the inner thighs. The elbows should remain outside or just above the pattern of movement, and the shoulders relaxed.

In the side-thrust kick, the kick should be delivered in a pattern directly from the side without leaning unnecessarily backwards between the point where the knee lifts in its primary motion and the impact point. With the side of the body facing the target, the knees should be lifted high, aligned with the area to be impacted. Before the kick is delivered, it is important to rotate the hips slightly in the direction of the target. This will angle the knee and foot to allow for a smooth thrusting motion. Again, there should be no feeling of separation between one leg and the other; the shoulders should continue to remain as upright as possible, moving in the direction of the target, and the hands should remain free and unrestricted.

In either case, the force is generated from the hip and base-leg, and one should be cautious not to over-extend or separate the weapon from its supportive structure.

In punching, it is important to relax the shoulders and keep the weapon centered. The pulling-hand should be as strong as the punching hand. The projection of the punch should not be outside of the front knee, and the head and hips should be on a similar vertical plane. One should practice to get the hips through the target as if the extended arms were but projections from a vertical surface.

. . . use the practice for crossing the void. Instead of seeing the target as the point of the triangle, place the fist at that point.

"Better indeed is knowledge than mechanical practice. Better than knowledge is meditation. But better still is surrender of attachment to results, because there follows immediate peace."
—The Way of Love from *The Bhagavad Gita*

In the course of time, as one studies the nature of war, one discovers a method of peace. When such is discovered, one has become that for which one was seeking and the warrior becomes a priest.

THE THREAD

Meditation is the key,
  nothing else makes sense
without it.

                        —Guru Dorjie

When we speak of warriors,
we are simply speaking of a
way of life without the buffers
of any personal or rational
justification for being, or excuses
for existence.

When we speak of war,
we are speaking of
impeccable honesty in
the face of one's own
shadows, and persistence
on the path toward
enlightenment.

We are not speaking of
infringement upon the
lives of others nor mechanical
contest to determine who is
strongest or bravest ... no, we
are speaking of countless
encounters with our own
unconsciousness and the mental
clarity to persist upon the
journey towards understanding
with fortitude and priority.

When we speak of attainment,
we speak of a peace
which can never achieved by
simply killing one's opponent;
we we speak of a freedom which is
contained in the unity that
binds all humanity into a single cell
of radiant intelligence.

> ... the ultimate mystery is
> the mystery of "Self."
> What is it that we preserve
> on the battle field, if still
> this mystery persists?

Becoming The Practice

What is heaven that we
can not achieve it through
peaceful coexistence?

But as men, we have
not achieved such a lofty
state of being. There are
things we want, and
are willing to take ... there
are things that we
have that we are not willing
to be without.

We remain the victims—
possessed by what we have
and intimidated by those
things that we can not possess.

And, our practice continues!

> "One day, going to practice
> will not make any difference, for
> you will have become It."
> —A cook who studied Taek Wan Do

I do not teach karate,
I attempt to help students
develop a rhythm which
is natural and instinctive,
and a perspective of self
which is characterized by a
respect for others.

These things, I believe, are
best taught through basics.

There were times in the past
when free-fighting played an
important role in my practice.
Now, I am beginning to
appreciate the simplicity of
basics ... they have a certain
purity which reminds me
of a mentality which is
not complicated, like the
single cutting edge of a
well honed katana.

We travel alone . . .
though in the company of others

1965 . . . A sergeant in the Marine Corps, stationed at MCAS El Toro, I had just returned from Okinawa and realized that Viet Nam was fast becoming the nexus of our national morality, the "killing field"of ethical human and social relationships.

As a matter of conscience, I could only object to what was for me a contradiction to all that was good in America—a final blow to our integrity as a "nation indivisible . . . ."

And, who am I if I cannot live by my own principles, or die if necessary . . . alone.

> " . . . I understand that the rules of
> combat have not changed since
> neolithic times. In but particles of
> a second, one must be able to
> abandon our Twentieth-Century humanity
> and return to the essence of one's
> Being."
> —An unknown Shaman

A Balanced Perspective

"The idea behind doing kata
is to break through a barrier ...
we have to confront our own
feelings every time.

> Yet, knowing our own
> feelings is just one half
> of the equation.

We must also see
the other half ...
we must also see
nature—the beauty
of the day, the shinning sun,
the trees and the flowers...."

—From a training session
with Mr. Ohshima

Through meditation I have witnessed a
state of mind which incorporated the body,
but which was not hindered by it ...
a sort of fluid state ... the body seemed
to float as a leaf upon a current of wind.

Such experiences where usually
linked to practices of breathing.

The practice of the martial arts and that
of yoga have some common characteristics.
Most important is the relationship
between form and breath.

A simple illustration might suffice
for those who have not experienced
this phenomenon:

Sit quietly in an open space, gaze
into the distance without straining your
eyes, and pay attention to your breathing.

Ten minutes should be
a sufficient amount of time to
recognize a difference in your
state of awareness.

> "Meditation is the key!
> Nothing else makes
> sense without it."
> —Guru Dorjie

Time And Potential

I am not the creator of
this art that I practice ...
It is through the practice of
the art and close scrutiny of
my actions as a person, that
I have become more aware of a
creative process.

There ... there is
the role of my teachers!
They help me to
refine that which is
becoming.

Neither they, nor I
can know the fruits
of our labor. So,
our loyalties to one
another are not for the
sake of what has been ...
but rather for the sake
of what could be

... given the context of
our mutual potential, and time.

        ... who among us can gauge
      the heart of the eternal, or know
        the soul of a fellow-man?

States of Awareness ...

Posture and attitude
are reflections of states
of awareness.

when one's posture is altered,
there is an immediate change in
one's attitude.

In yoga the psychological and
physiological changes which
result from countless hours
in the lotus position are often
defined as states of awareness.
In the martial arts those changes
are perceived as levels of
emotional and technical mastery ...
sort of a mentality.

The difference is in approach, and the
perception of the Way. All experiences
are anchored in the Essence Being of the
Universe. Our training is only our
disciplined effort at demonstrating
the unity between humanity and
Creative Causality.

When karate was first exposed to the masses, it had an almost
mystical image—more than a few persons spoke of the "Secret
Teachings of Karate-do."

Much of this mystique was rooted in ignorance and could be reduced to technical theory and application. But in essence, there are secrets of the art which remain so . . . they are part and parcel of the Universal Secret Doctrine and have little or nothing to do with one's fighting skills, but everything to do with one's experience in Being.

The Tao that can be told is not the eternal Tao;
The name that can be named is not the eternal Name.
The Nameless is the Source of Heaven and Earth;
The named is the Mother of the Ten Thousand Things.
Desireless, one may behold the mystery;
Desiring, one may see the manifestations.
Though one in origin,
They emerge with distinct names.
Both are mysteries—
Depth within depth—
The threshold of all secrets.

—Tao Te Ching

押

"There are three
levels to consider
when working with
beginners: The first
level is push!
The second level
is push!
The third level
is push!

Still, pulling
is important."

—Note from
a practice with Mr. Ohshima

Reflections...

I sat in zazen ... my mind restless, reflecting on a subtle concept which became more clear as I sank into the center of myself— What place is this? In its clarity I cannot see. Its transparency of thought and being is meaningless to my rationalization ... my mind is swept into silence of its own accord and the countless things to be thought of are one thing which can not be defined. I became still.

The moment we bow I am catapulted back into a timeless space. I am here now ... in the presence.

In exercise I am aware of the common breath which weaves the group together. My body responds to the dynamics of this breathing and the muscles warm-up in anticipation of its confrontation with the mind.

We face each other for one-time encounter. He will attack. I will defend. I sink into my stillness, back to a place where nothing exists and give myself to an action which is not precipitated by an act ... a concept which does not win, or loose ... a thoughtlessness which reflects thinking, but is not entangled by the thoughts.

I hear the silence, the high-pitched humming of the atmosphere, as he begin to come out of himself and attack. Pressing forward to enter his center my mind implodes upon itself ... I am no longer in my body. I "see" the dynamics of his weapon —right hand, right foot in synchronicity, his eyes focused, his hips pushing hard into his attack!

Through some strange process, in fractions of a second, as if projected on a gigantic video screen, I have a clear picture of both of us. I see my back. He is moving in slow motion towards me and I have a full frontal view...including the tie of the belt and the movement of his gi.

I block and counter in slow motion with a kiai. Someone yells, "yame," and the confrontation ends. My entire body is tingling. My mind is alert, conscious of the movie that I have just seen.

> ...We are, after all but shadows of
> our greater selves.

"We place emphasis on
getting low to teach
a mentality."

—Note from
a session with Mr. Ohshima

教師弟

A Concept of Humanity

The expansion of self
into the selfless is an
apparent contradiction
to the Practice of the
martial arts. Yet
it appears to be the
gateway to understanding
our unconscious intent.

It is easy to equate such
a transition with states of
denial or self-sacrifice.
... that is before understanding
that the whole of humanity
is at stake. Every act,
and all actions are interwoven—
they are separate only as
isolated observations.

Humanity is only separate
in concept. As a whole it
is a singular moving force.

Each relationship ... each
encounter is important in
view of the whole.

A one-armed boxer can be
a peerless foe, or a loyal
friend.

The Primordial Vastness is the
sky, the Primordial Vastness is
the sphere of space; the Primordial
Vastness is the mother, the father,
the son; the Primordial Vastness is
all the gods, the five sorts of
men, all that was born
and shall be born.
—Rig Veda

When facing an opponent, one becomes aware of feelings which translate into concepts that dictate reflective actions.

Calmness is not non-feeling... it is disentanglement from feelings, a clearness which is not disturbed by circumstance.

"The inseparableness of all living things is as natural as it is inescapable."
—- The Tibetan Book of The Great Liberation

Strength
... It is not the muscles alone!

It is not the muscles alone,
but the whole form as
it lends to an attitude
which the mind and body
adopts....

Reflect upon this idea:

If all things evolve from the
inside out, is true strength
outside, or is it inside?

The warrior or the
priest discovers
only the power to
imagine and live in
personal harmony.

One learns through an
absolute faith in the Divine,
the other through the
infallibility instincts of the
Spirit.

Each journey begins
with the desire to
understand, and each
ends with a greater desire
for knowledge, a mature
compassion for other
beings and a silent
acknowledgement of
the Unknowable but
Perfect Cause for
Life.

In the beginning of our training
we acknowledge a greater presence in
life which we defer to the teacher.

When practice has become a way
of life we acknowledge an even greater
presence ... life Itself.

... the teacher's knowledge
transferred to the student in
acts of training are the Rites of
Passage. ...

This, most of society has lost.
This is tradition ... father to son,
mother to daughter, teacher to
student, senior to junior,
guru to disciple, the Creator
to the Created. ...

These are the foot prints on the
path of life, the leaves on a
tree: two of the three jewels.
The third is Truth.

... these things we learn from the teacher,
practice as a student, and live as Martial Artists.

生死

It's like dying...

It is not for ourselves alone
that we practice karate-do...
It is for all sentient beings.

The dogma of systems and
masters warrants close
scrutiny...there have been
few wars which were not
fought in the name of a
god or a master.

All too often, a belt becomes
a banner, the instructor
a god and the student a
master...at least of vanity
and self deceit.

Mastery is a transcendental
existence...close to dying—
Maybe it is more like dying
to all the things that most
men live for.

> —Reflections on a conversation
> with Shimabuku Eizo—1963

Time and experience have demonstrated how powerful and inspiring the life experience can be.

A countless number of opportunities co-exist in each moment!

Discipline and refined attention are tools which can give each of us the clearness and vision to unleash the moment-to-moment potential which becomes our futures, the futures of our families and friends, and the future of our world community.

This is the real value of Karate-do—the esoteric teachings.

As we sharpen our technique and refine our fighting strategies, we should remember:

> the objective of training in any discipline is to understand certain principles, and to become proficient in their application.

Lineage of Author
Shorin Ryu/Shotokan Karate Heritage

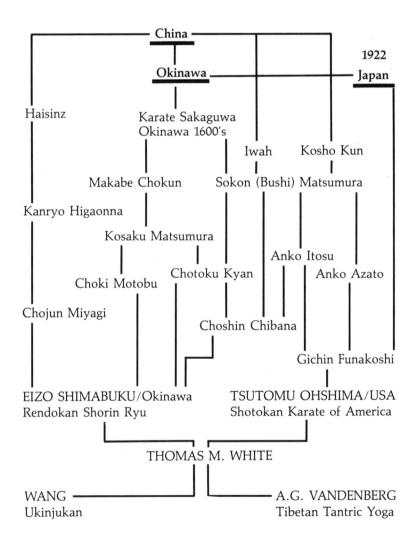